A Slave Girl's Story.

PREPARED FOR PUBLICATION
BY
HISTORIC PUBLISHING
Edited by Historic Publishing
©2017

A Slave Girl's Story.
Being an Autobiography of Kate Drumgoold
By
Kate Drumgoold
©1898

CONTENTS

A
Slave Girl's Story.
BEING AN AUTOBIOGRAPHY OF
Kate Drumgoold.

BROOKLYN-NEW YORK.
©1898.

A Slave Girl's Story.

A SLAVE GIRL'S STORY.

CHAPTER I.

ONCE a slave girl, I have endeavored to fill the pages with some of the most interesting thoughts that my mind is so full of, and not with something that is dry.

This sketch is written for the good of those that have written and prayed that the slaves might be a freed people, and have schools and books and learn to read and write for themselves; and the Lord, in His love for us and to us as a race, has ever found favor in His sight, for when we were in the land of bondage He heard the prayers of the faithful ones, and came to deliver them out of the Land of Egypt.

For God loves those that are oppressed, and will save them when they cry unto him, and when they put their trust in Him.

Some of the dear ones have gone to the better land, but this is one of the answers to their prayers.

We, as the Negro Race, are a free people, and God be praised for it. We, as the Negro Race, need to feel proud of the race, and I for one do with all my heart and soul and mind, knowing as I do, for I have labored for the good of the race, that their children might be the bright and shining lights. And we can see the progress that we are making in an educational way in a short time, and I think that we should feel very grateful to God and those who are trying to help us forward. God bless such with their health, and heart full of that same love, that this world cannot give nor taketh away.

There are many doors that are shut to keep us back as a race, but some are opened to us, and God be praised for those that are opened to the race, and I hope that they will be true to their trust and be of the greatest help to those that have given them a chance.

There are many that have lost their lives in the far South in trying to get an education, but there are many that have done well, and we feel like giving God all the praise.

I was born in Old Virginia, in or near the Valley, the other side of Petersburg, of slave parents, and I can just call to mind the time when the war began, for I was not troubled then about wars, as I was feeling as free as anyone could feel, for I was sought by all of the rich whites of the neighborhood, as they all loved me, as noble whites will love a child, like I was in those days, and they would send for me if I should be at my play and have me to talk for them, and all of their friends learned to love me and send me presents, and I would stand and talk and preach for some time for them.

My dear mother was sold at the beginning of the war, from all of her little ones, after the death of the lady that she belonged to, and who was so kind to my dear mother and all of the rest of the negroes of the place; and she never liked the idea of holding us as slaves, and she always said that we were all that she had on the earth to love; and she did love me to the last.

The money that my mother was sold for was to keep the rich man from going to the field of battle, as he sent a poor white man in his stead, and should the war end in his favor, the poor white man should have given to him one negro, and that would fully pay for all of his service in the army. But my God moves in a way unknown to men, and they can never understand His ways, for He can plant His footsteps on the North, the South, the East, the West, and outride any man's ideas; and how wonderful are all of his ways. And if we, as a race, will only put our trust in Him, we shall gain the glorious victory, and be a people whose God is the God of all this broad earth, and may we humble ourselves before Him and call Him, Blessed.

I told you that my white mother did not like the idea of calling us her slaves, and she always prayed God that I should never know what slavery was, for she said I was never born to serve as did the slaves of some of the people that owned them.

And God, in His love for me and to me, never let me know of it, as did some of my own dear sisters, for some of them were hired out after, the old home was broken up.

My mother was sold at Richmond, Virginia, and a gentleman bought her who lived in Georgia, and we did not know that she was sold until she was gone; and the saddest thought was to me to know which way she had gone and I used to go outside and look up to see if there was anything that would direct me, and I saw a clear place in the sky, and it seemed to me the way she had gone, and I watched it three and a half years, not knowing what that meant, and it was there the whole time that mother was gone from her little ones.

On one bright Sunday I asked my older sister to go with me for a nice walk and she did so, for she was the one that was so kind to the rest of us--and we saw some sweet flowers on the wayside and we began to have delight in picking them, when all at once I was led to leave her alone with the flowers and to go where I could look up at that nice, clear spot, and as I wanted to get as near to it as I could, I got on the fence, and as I looked that way I saw a form coming to me that looked like my dear mother's, and calling to my sister Frances to come at once and see if that did not look like my dear mother, and she came to us, so glad to see us, and to ask after her baby that she was sold from that was only six weeks old when she was taken from it; and I would that the whole world could have seen the joy of a mother and her two girls on that heaven-made day--a mother returning back to her own once more, a mother that we did not know that we should ever see her face on this earth more. And mother, not feeling good over the past events, had made up her mind that she would take her children to a part of this land where she thought that they would never be in bondage any more on this earth.

So she sought out the headman that was placed there by the North to look after the welfare of lately emancipated negroes of the

South, to see that they should have their rights as a freed people.

This gentleman's name was Major Bailley, who was a gentleman of the highest type, and it was this loving man that sent my dear mother and her ten little girls on to this lovely city, and the same time he informed the people of Brooklyn that we were on the way and what time we should reach there; and it seemed as though the whole city were out to meet us. And as God would have it, six of us had homes on that same day, and the people had their carriages there to take us to our new homes.

This God-sent blessing was of a great help to mother, as she could get the money to pay her rent, which was ten dollars per month, and God bless those of my sisters who could help mother to care for her little ones, for they had not been called home then, and God be praised for all that we have ever did for her love and comfort while she kept house.

The subject was only a few years old, when she saw her heart so fixed that she could not leave me at my mother's any longer, so she took me to be her own dear, loving child, to eat, drink, sleep and to go wherever she went, if it was for months, or even years; I had to be there as her own and not as a servant, for she did not like that, but I was there as her loving child for her to care for me, and everything that I wanted I had; truly do I feel grateful to my Heavenly Father for all of those blessings that came to me in the time that I needed so much of love and care.

This dear lady, Mrs. Bettie House, my white mother, died at the beginning of the war and then the time came for poor me to go to my own dear mother again for a while, and soon the time came for us to be parted asunder, where we did not see one another anymore until after the war of 1865. And we all thought that mother was dead, for we did not hear any tidings of her after she had reached the far South.

I shall never forget that lovely Sunday morning when I saw my dear mother returning again to her own native home and her own dear ones once more, but mother would not go to the house with us, as she did not want to take the law in her own hands. So she told sister and I where she was stopping and told us to come to her after we had told the gentleman where we lived, and I went to him and told him that mother had come back and wanted to have us to come where she was staying. He, Mr. House, did not want us to go, and I took my oldest sister and marched out to go where mother was and he did not like that freedom, and he tried to find which way that we had gone to the place, but he did not find us, and we had been to the place where the people were that had homes, and that they would kill us at first sight, and that was all that I wanted to see, and I did not find one thing true of their sayings.

Mother now has to tell the gentleman where to find all of her own dear ones whom God in His love for had kept for her, and she should have been very grateful to Him that her life had been prolonged and all that she had left alive were still alive, awaiting for her to return, and finding that her children were all over in different places, and now she has to tell where to find them, through the help of the Lord. And when she had gone for them and was told that some of her own were dead, she said that she would go and dig up their bones; but they were not dead, as was said, and she sent the soldiers after them and sometimes they were told the same as mother was, and some of the little ones had to be sent for two or three times before they were brought. My oldest sister knew where they all were, so she could help to get the rest.

One of my sisters who lived at the same place where we were living was detained and the soldiers had go three times before they could get her, for they said that she had died since we had left, for I would not stay at the place as he, Mr. House, did not want us to go on Monday to see my mother, on whom I should look to, as she had come to claim her own. I told my oldest sister that we would leave, and my sister Annie was at one of Mr. House's sons, who found that we were going to see mother and she came with us, so that left three there yet; that was sister Lavinia and the baby, sister Rosa, and they let mother have the baby, as it was a sickly child; and she had to send there three times before she could get sister Lavinia, and the last time the soldiers, with horses, went, and the House's took off all of her clothing and put them into water to keep them from taking her, and they had to take blankets and wrap her in them, and bring her to mother, and she took sick from that time from the long ride, and getting cold she nearly died.

One they hid in the garden; one they put in the cellar, and so these were hard times for mother and us, who were in the road one night walking to find some place to get out of the rain and let those wet garments get dried, for it was so dark that we could not see a hand before us.

But after all the hard trials we reached this lovely city, where there are those that love and fear God, and who love the souls of the negro as well as those of the white, the red, the yellow or brown races of the earth, for we have ever found some of the people who do not forget us day or night in their prayers, that God will send a blessing to us as a race.

To my story of a life of slavery:

My dear mother had a dear husband that she was sold from also, and he, not knowing that he should ever see my mother any more, as the times were then, he waited for a while and then he found him another wife, and when mother came and found that he was married to another she tried to get him, but she could do nothing about it; so having to leave him behind to look after the last one and her family, although it seemed hard for her to do so.

My mother had a large family to take care of, but the Lord was good to her and helped her, for she had laid some of them away, and then there were ten little girls to care for. My brother was lost to us and to mother also, as he was sent to the war to do service for his owner, and we did not know if he was alive or not, and he was my mother's only boy, as this is a girl family that you do not see or hear of every day, for that made seventeen girls to have battle through life had they all have lived to this time,

CHAPTER II.

MY mother did not know where my brother was before she was sold, for we heard that he had tried to get over to the Northern side and had been taken to Richmond, Va., and put into Castle Thunder, and that was the last that we heard of him during the war. When, to our surprise, we were on our way North we learned that he was going to school; that the Northern people had teachers there in the South to teach them to read and to write; and he learning that we had gone North made himself ready and came on, but he did not know where to find us, so getting a place to work, and the same time telling those that he worked for that his people were here somewhere, they found mother and got her to go to the place where he was, and sure enough there was her dead and lost boy, and the joy and love that came to that dear, loving mother and her only son on that day will never be known on this side of the grave, as they have both gone to the land of the blest, for my brother never used any bad language in his life, and when he took the Lord for his own, it was his meat and his drink to live for Him and to follow where He led, and he died a true child of the King.

A few years later and mother's name was enrolled in the Lambs' Book of Life, for she gladly answered to the roll call and fell asleep in the arms of Jesus.

Well, my first place was in Adelphi street, with a family by the name of Hammond, and I was there to help do the work, and when they found that I liked to work so well they wanted me to do so much that I left that place and got me another, for I did not get out to church or to Sunday-school, and that was not the way that I had been trained, for when I was three years old my white mother had taken me to church with her on horseback.

Well, I said that I saw these children going to school on every weekday but Saturdays and on Sundays to Sunday school, and I there at work as if it were not the Lord's day, and I never shall like to work on that day as I was born on Sunday morning.

Well, I left there not knowing what to do, and a white lady took me in and told me to stay there until I could get another place, and I helped her girl on the next day to finish all of the work and I made ready to look for a place, and God did help me to find one and I shall never forget Him as long as I live, for that was with a fine family and they showed me love at once and I showed them love in return.

They were members of the Washington Avenue Baptist Church, and a more beloved family never lived. This was the Bailley family-- Mr. and Mrs. Bailley, Miss Abbey Bailley, Mr. Bailley's sister, a young lady in her teens, Miss Ella Bailley, and a nice boy by the name of Johnny Bailley, and they were a nice family and they took me to church on Sunday morning and sent me to Sunday-school in in the afternoon with their children, and what a heaven it seemed to me from the place where I was living at first.

I shall always remember my dear white mother, of whom I spoke of in the first part, and whom I shall call your attention to in many more pages of this little Life Book, and shall always remember her with love and the kindest feeling. She was a member of the true Methodist Church and was never seen by her darling child from the House of God since I could remember, for I was with her at all times on the family horse, Kimble, and when I got large enough to ride alone she bought me a fine black that had all the metal that a horse could have, and his name was Charlie Engrum, and she paid a large price for him, and he was the grandest horse I ever saw, and it was my

20

delight to be near a horse or horses when I
was a child, for I did not have any fear of any
kind of horse, and I would take a ride the first
thing in the morning, even before I would have
my breakfast, and my dear white mother would
save it for me as she knew that I would have
that ride first, for it always made her feel proud
to see how well I had learned to ride, and she
was the one that had taught me how to ride, for
she had me on the horse when I was three
years old and from that time until she went
home to come out no more forever.

I was two and a half years, as near as I
can remember, when my own slave mother's
house was burned to the ground, and I shall
never forget that Saturday night. My mother's
husband had gone to a dance and mother was
there alone with her little ones, and we all
came near getting burned up. We were all
asleep when I awoke and found the house in a
blaze. I did not know enough or I was so much
scared that I did not call to my mother, but I
think that she heard me when I rolled out of the
bed, and she was out of the bed quick as could
be and getting the feather beds she threw them
out of the door and got the children and threw
them out, and she, finding that she did not
have them all, said, "My God! I have not all of
my little ones;" and she ran in the house to look
and she found me under the bed, for I saw so

much fire that I was getting out of it, and God be praised that I was saved from that fire, and I have not had the time to run after any fires since, for that fire was all the fire I want.

I had not to stay there then, for the time is near at hand when I shall go to my white mother's to live, for she is in Tennessee and will come home soon to be with her darling child; and when she shall start again I shall go, and now the times are all well for me as then, but the time has come that the Lord has called her away from her child to be with Him, and how could I live without her? And she was to leave her sick child there for her own mother to care for, and God will raise up friends in this lonely world to look after those that cry unto heaven, believing that He is a hearer of the true prayer. I shall always remember that Saturday afternoon when I was lying so sick when my dearly beloved white mother took so sick, and they had the doctor there for me, and he had to see after her the same time, and she was getting so much worse all the time and the doctor had not any hopes of her, and they took me from the room where she was, to a room upstairs and she had them to take me down to look at her once more. That was on Sunday and on Monday she heard the call to her to come up to that blessed land where she should be forever with the Lord and her dear husband.

A Slave Girl's Story

What a glory it must be for those that have washed their robes and made them white in the blood of the Lamb.

I can call to mind when she the blessed one, that I call my white mother, went to get me some shoes and a fine hat, and the one that sold them told her, as she looked at a hat I wanted, that its price was twenty dollars, but I was not thinking of the prices then as I do now, and I cried to have that hat and did not want any of the others, and he told my white mother that was too much for to spend on a hat for me, but she told him nothing would cost too much for her to get for me, and she got that fine hat for me and he had his money; so you can see how much she loved me. And now that dear one is gone from me, and it seemed the dearest one on this earth, and I did not think then that I could have lived without her whom God had given to me for this world, but God, in His wonderful love for me and to me, raised up friends for me and helped me to find favor in the sight of all the people, for they seemed to love me for her sake, and I did not get well for a long time.

This subject came to this dear lady, Mrs. Bettie House, when but three years old, and from the day she came to that house she walked in her footsteps, for she, Mrs. House,

could not move, but she was right in the way;
and when she used to set me down for my play
at certain times in the day, when she was
going in her room for prayer, she would find me
near before she was through; and if ever there
was a loving woman she was one, and I owe
my love to God for such a one as she was to
care for me all of those nights of watching by
my bed, while the angels watched from above
to see that I should rise from that bed and live
to be a woman that would live for God and
bless His name in all the earth, knowing that I
am tempted and tried on every hand. But
trusting in His omnipotent power I shall reach
the land of the blest where that dear one has
gone to come out no more forever.

Well, to my story:

Dear public, hoping that this little life will
be read with the greatest love for humanity,
and I am sure that if you have any love for the
God of heaven you cannot fail to find a love for
this book, and I hope you will find a fullness of
joy in reading this life, for if your heart was like
a stone you would like to read this little life.

I had many a hard spell of sickness since
the death of this lady and the doctors said that
I could not live beyond a certain time, but every
time they said so Doctor Jesus said she shall

24

live, for because I live she shall live also; and He came to me and laid His strong arm around me and raised me up by the power of His might, and to see the salvation of our God in the land of the living. And to-day I can praise His name for His wonderful love to the children of man.

I told you that my brother was the oldest child of eighteen and he was in his teens when he was sent to the war; and it was a great thing to him when he found himself in the hands of a people that were so kind and good to him and showing such love for him, after being knocked around by those he had been staying with, and it seemed like a heaven to him; and he did learn fast, and he felt so glad to learn to read and to write, and he would sit at nights when he was through with his daily toil and write, so that he could let someone look at it and see how well he was getting along, and I saw how anxious he was to get an education. I asked my lady to let him come there and wait on the table, and have time to go every day to school, and she did so, and he would go to No. 1 School to Mr. C. Dosey, and he did nicely in his studies, and God be praised that he had that much to take home with him, and I shall always feel glad that I gave him that much.

I was thinking of my dear brother when
the news reached me that he was in this city,
and I can never tell anyone how glad that I was
to see the only boy that my mother ever had,
for we all loved him dearly, as he cared for all
the rest of the children and it was no more than
natural that we should; and my mother thought
so much of him that she often would say if we
were all boys she would not have to worry, for
boys could do so much better than girls. But I
think that she found that the girls were the best
in her old age, for if one could not be near her
the other would, and if there is a time in the life
of a parent it is when they are helpless, and a
boy is not any good to care for a sick parent
and they have to go without care.

But God be praised for all of the love and
honor that was bestowed on mother before she
went home, for God has told us to honor our
fathers and our mothers that their days may be
long upon the land which the Lord, thy God,
giveth thee; and we cannot do them enough
honor for the love and the all-night watching
that we have when we are babies, and if we
have all of the love and care that I had, I am
sure that a mother has her hands full; and
when now I think of the care and the worry that
it was to take care of my sick body. I cannot
help telling someone of it, that they may feel as
grateful as I feel, for God did give them love for

me, and if there is one that should feel grateful it is this feeble-bodied slave girl, for I was such a slave to sickness, and God was so good to raise me, even me, and I will say, praise His name.

I was telling you of my white mother being so true to the attendance in the services of God, and I only wish that you could have known her as I did, for she was more like one of the heavenly host than she was like us, who are such sinful creatures. Now, it seems like sometimes that we have not much love for the One who had so much love for us that He gave all the dear One, that He had to bring us to Himself, that we should taste of those joys which He has for those who have washed their robes and made them white in the Blood of the Lamb.

The Lord helped me to find love and favor with all after my white mother was gone from this earth, when I felt that I would soon follow the darling one to the blessed mansion; and I would look to see her come to me, and I went as soon as I was well to the house and lay on the steps, and it was not until we had left the dear old place before I could be kept from there; and I wish that the whole world could have seen how much she was like an angel, and I would to God she could see me to-day; it would do you good. Lord, lead me on day by day, and help my feeble life to be formed like her's, for when I think how she used to watch by my bed at nights, while the angels watched by my bed from on high to see that I should rise; and is not God the One that I should serve? And I love to serve Him and honor Him, for He is my all in all; for she has shown me how great her love was for me and all of humanity, and I love to think of her love and to know how wonderful it would be to see her sweet face on this green earth, and it does seem to me as if I could almost see her by thinking of her so much.

I have said that we came to this lovely city in the year of our Lord 1865, and in that year I went to live with a good family that were members of the church, where the Lord spoke peace to my soul, under the preaching of the Rev. David Moore, then the beloved leader of the noblest band of God's children on this earth and a more beloved people never lived. They were always on the lookout for any strangers that might come in the church, and they soon found me out as I was a stranger in the Monday night meeting. The dear pastor came to me the first one, for he did not stop to think whether I was an African or what nation I had come from, but he saw in me a soul, and he wanted to find out if there was any room for

Jesus to live or what I should do with Jesus, or
what should I do for Him, who had done so
much for me; and my poor heart was ready
and waiting for someone to come to its rescue.
It was then and there that I yielded my life and
my all to the one that can save to the uttermost
all that come unto Him by the Lord Jesus
Christ.

I followed my Lord and Master in the
Jordan in the year of our Lord 1866, and those
sweet moments have never left me once. As
the years go by they seem to be the more
sweet to my sinful soul, and I am trying to wing
my way to these bright mansions above, where
I shall meet those dear ones who have gone
before.

I have had some of the darkest days of
my life while on this voyage of life, but when it
is dark Jesus says, "Peace, be still and fear
not, for I will pilot thee."

And then my heart can sing:

"Jesus, Savior, pilot me
 Over life's tempestuous sea,
 Unknown waves before me roll,
 Hiding rocks and treacherous shoals,

Chart and compass come from Thee,
Jesus, Savior, pilot me."

I know that He has led me through paths
seen and unseen and has been my pilot, for
we have been called to pass through many a
dark trial, but God has been able for it all.

My dear mother had four of her children
called home to heaven within a short time.
Some of them left her for the land of love in the
same month, and there seemed like nothing
but God's displeasure on us, but it was God's
love to us, for we know that they are safe from
all harm and danger in this world of sin and
distress. Some of them I never saw more after
landing in this city, but I shall see them and
know them when I shall have fought the
blessed battle on this side, and the victory shall
be on the Lord's side. Then I can sing with the
angels above:

"Crown Him, Crown Him, angels,
Crown Him, Crown Him King of Kings,
Crown Him, Crown Him, angels, Crown Him,
Crown Him, Crown the Savior King of Kings."

What joy there will be to crown Him as our
Heavenly King and to know that we are the
inhabitants of that kingdom.

CHAPTER III.

I WAS baptized by the Rev. David Moore, the pastor of the Washington Avenue Church, who is one of the best beloved ones on this earth, for he never overlooked me in the time that my soul needed the Lord Jesus Christ to save me from my sins and make me a child of the King, which makes me what I am today. I bless God that he ever put it in my dear mother's mind to come to this place, for she was not a Christian, and the heaviest burden that I have carried was praying for one that was the head of the great family where she should have been a leader of her dear ones to the Lamb of God, that taketh away the sins of the world. But God be praised for a little one to lead so many, for of all the people of mothers, there was not one that knew of this love of God, and how many were the souls given for me to work for. I told my mother that I had found Jesus and was going to follow Him. She said, "My child, you are too young, I am afraid that you will not hold out." And I said, "Mother, if I should look to myself I should fail, but I look to Jesus. I have given my life and He can hold me in the power of His might and can keep me from failing; so I cannot go against your will, but I must follow Him, for you know how He has saved me from sickness so many times, and now the time has come for me to pay my vows unto Him for making me His own." I went forward in the way that He marked out for me and then to pray that she might be saved.

My grandma was almost one hundred years old, and when she heard that the Lord had saved me and that I was praying for her she saw her own sins and asked me to come on to visit all of my people, and I, getting ready, got my oldest sister to go with me. I found that the way was opened for work, as there we began the work, and they were looking to see something that they would never see in this world, and sweetly they were all brought to the Savior. Grandma went home to carry the good news and some of the rest have gone with the same good news.

Later years some of my sisters came and some did not come. Then some got tired and went back to the world, but I have no joy like the joy there is in the Lord.

My dear mother found the peace in Jesus before she went to that land of song. When the Lord sent the death angel to call her name she was ready to answer, "Here am I ready to go in, to come out no more."

My mother left us on the 28th day of February, 1894, in the triumph of faith in the

Lord Jesus Christ. What a blessed thought that I shall soon be with her on the other side of the river to help her "Crown Him Lord of all."

To my story:

The subject of this sketch, as I said, was born again under the preaching of Rev. David Moore, of the Washington Avenue Baptist Church, which is one of the noblest churches of this city, and it has some of the best people in it of any church in the world, for there is more done for those in need in other lands. When I became a member of that church, I could not read in any book, for I did not know a letter. There was a gentleman in the church by the name of Mr. Lansberry, who finding that I was one of those that was going to learn, went to a store and bought me a First Reader and gave it to me, and I did not lose any of my time at nights. I went to the meetings every night and came back and got a lady, who was a sister of Mr. Bailey, to be my teacher, and sometimes she used to be so very sleepy that she could not keep her eyes open and I would shake her and say that my lesson was to be learned, and it was always well learned. Then I went to the Sunday school to let my Sunday-school teacher hear it on Sundays, and he, Mr. Ward, always said that he was sure that I would learn so fast I would soon catch up with his Bible Class. It was not long before I could lay my Reader down and take my lessons in the Bible, and I can bless God for all of this, for the love and the kindness that I received of all that knew me was a token of His great love for me, and I know that He was near me all the time to bring me nearer to the Light. My mind was then fixed that I should someday go to school and I could not rest night or day I was so anxious, to go to school; but my dear mother could not send me. She had poor health and no one to help her to take care of the younger children, and I had to work and do the best I could with my books, hoping that the time would come that I should see myself sitting in some school studying, the same time asking mother to let two of the other children go to school every day. She did let them go for a while, but someone came and wanted her to let them go to work out again and she let them go out to work.

Well, I said that I would go to school someday, and they had a fine time laughing at my high ideas and I let them laugh all that they wanted to, but I worked hard and long to get the means that I might be able to go, as I said, to some pay school, where I could not be stopped at any time. When I was almost ready to leave for some school the smallpox took me, and I was laid aside for three or four years; that is, I was not well, and thought that my plans were all broken. I still trusted in God, for I knew that He would do all things for me as long as I put my trust in Him.

Well, as time rolled on I found myself improving slowly and I was then living with a dear, good lady by the name of Miss L. A. Pousland, who is one of the loveliest ladies that ever lived, for she loves me to-day as a mother, though she is in eightieth odd year and is doing well for an old lady.

We were living in South Oxford street when I took sick of the smallpox and she did not want me taken away from there, as she wanted to take care of me herself, but I felt that it would be too much for her to wait on me, so the doctor said that it was only a heavy cold that I had taken and would be all right in a week or so. But I knew that I had a fever of some kind, so I asked that I might go to my mother's house, and she sent for the carriage and I went home.

When I had reached my mother's I felt somewhat better, only to grow worse all the time, and my eyes getting so that I could not see when it was day or night. I had a nurse that knew all about the disease and a good doctor that the city health doctor let take charge of the

case after he had been out there to see me;
and knowing that the case was taking, that no
one should get it he let me remain at home for
nine days, and then I went to the hospital and
was there till the symptoms were well dried.

When the doctor found out that I was able
to come out he, Dr. Schenck, wrote to my lady
to send a carriage out. She did so at once and
I was at my mother's for a while, and then my
lady came to see me and told me how the
woman did the people in the house so I told
her how bad my limbs were, and she said that
if I could go home with her and tell her what to
do, she would get on without the woman and
let her go. My mother made me ready in a little
while and I was soon at the dear old home, 344
Carlton avenue.

God be praised for the way he has led me
since, I was three years old until this day, for it
was His hand that taught me to remember all
of these long years. I have in my mind the time
at the old home when they put me on the fine
dressing table in front of the large mirror, while
the Rev. Mr. Walker baptized me in the name
of the Father and the Son and the Holy Ghost,
according to the Methodist tests in those days,
and I always thought that was to give me my
Christian name; but when the Lord had spoken
peace to my soul He led me to follow in his

footsteps, and I gladly followed Him to be buried to the world--that is, to be put out of sight, and that is what the word means. I have found it to be one of those times when the Father was pleased with His own dear beloved Son, and I know that He will be pleased whenever we do please Him, for God so loved the world of sinful men that He gave His only begotten Son that whosoever believeth in Him should have everlasting life, for God sent not His Son into the world to condemn it, but that through Him all might believe in Him and have everlasting life.

I wish that I could know that the whole world was receiving this life, and that we all could help to crown Him, as the angels are crowning Him, the King of Kings and Lord of Heaven and of this earth.

It is a blessed hope to know that God is love, and they that worship Him must worship Him in spirit and in truth.

I joined the church in 1866 and began to try and follow in this good old way that leads from earth to glory, and it has not always been a path of the sweetest flowers, but I have never failed to find my all in the Lord Jesus Christ.

He led me on day by day, and after a while I found that He had led me to go away from home that I might get ready for the work that my heart was so full of, for every time that I saw the newspaper there was some one of our race in the far South getting killed for trying to teach and I made up my mind that I would die to see my people taught. I was willing to go to prepare to die for my people, for I could not rest till my people were educated. Now they are in a fair way to be the people that God speaks of in the Holy Word, as He says that Ethiopia shall yet stretch forth her hand and all nations shall bow unto her. I long to see the day that the Ethiopians shall all bow unto God as the One that we should all bow unto, for it is to Him that we all owe our homage and to be very grateful to Him for our deliverance as a race. If we should fail to give him the honor due there would a curse come to us as a race, for we remember those of olden times were of the same descent of our people, and some of those that God honored most were of the Ethiopians, such as the Unica and Philop, and even Moses, the law-giver, was of the same seed.

And not long ago darkness hung over the face of this race and God moved upon the face of this dark earth and the light came forth.

How wonderfully solemn and yet grand are these inspired thoughts and words of a race whose God is so loving and forgiving, and we, contemplating the grand mystery of the world beyond this vale of tears, for God does preserve all that He has planted on this earth.

No subject can surely be a more delightful study than the history of a slave girl, and the many things that are linked to this life that man may search and research in the ages to come, and I do not think there ever can be found any that should fill the mind as this book.

This is a perfect representation of things as I can remember them, and to think how wonderful are these most beneficent streams of God's providence to all those of our race that have prayed that their loving children might feel the warm streams of an education flowing through every child. Tens of thousands of miles, North, South, West and East, God has thrown His mantle of love all around us, and it is that which should make us love and fear Him, who is able to destroy both soul and body; for His searching eye rests on all of the negro race, to see what use they are going to make of their time and talent, and I hope that nature will teach them that all of our talent belongs to the great God who gave us our being.

Nature awakens in our being a feeling that we must lay at His feet that we may get the blessed approval, for we are so changeable, but God is unchanging. He is omnipotent, and all else is transition. Yet God rules the oceans, the mountains, the valleys, and all that walks the broad earth.

Well, now I shall tell you something more of my working in the City of Brooklyn. I lived with the Bailey family the first year, and when they went away in the summer, as all of the rich used to do, I stayed in the house for the summer and they went across the ocean and were away for some time. The next year I did not like to stay in the house alone, so Mrs. Bailey got me a place with a nice friend of hers, and when she came home, thought that she was going to have me to come back to live with her but I stayed with her friend as there were but three in the family and the work was not hard, and it gave me more time to study, and Mrs. Stafford's son. Willie, was so glad to have me as his pupil that I had not any trouble to get my lessons ready for him. He went to school every day and he could not get through his head how it was that I could not go to school every day as he did. His mother told him how it was and his eyes would fill with tears and he would ask his mother and father to let him stay at home on Sundays to read the Bible to me while I should get the dinner ready, and they would let him stay, for he wanted to see me going to the House of God on Sundays as they did and was willing to have anything to eat that I might have the opportunity of attending the church and Sunday-school. His mother would let me go to the Sunday school on every Sunday, for they were good people and were of the kind that delighted in their help and they were members of the Church of The Messiah, and they were a very happy family. They did not think that anything was too good for my enjoyment and that is the reason that I stayed with them and did not go back to the lady as she wanted me to do. I could not tell which seemed to love me most, and then her son was so willing to teach me, as Miss Abbie Bailey had, so I made up mind that as I had more time there for study I would remain, and I had some of the best days of my life when I began to learn so fast, and he would bring me before his mother and father that they might hear me recite my lessons and see how well I was doing under him as my teacher. They felt the more glad to see how much he was interested in teaching me. Later on in years, I was taken sick with the smallpox and was carried away to the hospital. He was taken sick while I was away and his mother said that he would call for me about the last one on this earth, and she tried to find me, but she did not

know where I was for some time after his
death, and then she felt so bad to think that he
was gone and did not see me, for he always
loved to be with me that he might hear me
sing, as I was always on the wings of song if I
were at my work; and that is the way that I
have been all of my life.

When I got well of the smallpox, as I said,
I went back to the place where I was living
when I took the malady, and there I tried to
work, but was very feeble for a long time and
under the doctor's care all of the time and
spending more than I could make, for some of
the doctors charged me two dollars a visit, and
that will use up a poor person's earnings very
soon.

But all of this time I kept in mind the idea
that I should save every cent that I could that I
might send myself to school someday. That
day did come when it seemed as dark as any
night I had ever seen, when I should go away
to boarding school and spend that little and
should not have enough to finish; but I went,
taking the Lord as the guide of my life, and the
way began to grow bright before me and I
could see all the clouds rolling away and the
brightness shining forth. I went to Washington,
D. C., and entered the Wayland Seminary,
under the leadership of Professor G. M. P.

King, of Bangor, Maine, with his other teachers and professors under him; all of whom are a noble band of teachers. And the way the Lord did help me in my studies is a blessing to the dear ones that I had under me for the eleven years that I was in the schoolwork, and the way they progressed.

I said that I attended the Wayland Seminary for three years, of eight months, making it in all of my stay there twenty four months, which may seem long to some, but it seems short to me, though I am very glad that I had that much time there for it was a fountain of blessing to my soul.

I left Washington, D. C., in the year of 1878 and came to Brooklyn and went to work again to earn money to go off to school, and when I did go it was to another school in the Blue Ridge, Alleghany Mountains, where the very air of heaven seemed to fan the whole hill sides, and there never was a more lovely place on this earth for one to learn a lesson, for we could see the key to all lessons where nature had designed for a grand school of learning. At this place was to be found one of the best schools of learning that has been built by man. And I think of the hundreds and thousands of teachers and preachers and lawyers and doctors that these two schools have turned out in the different parts of this country, and many of them are in other parts of the world.

And all of this has been done through the churches, and God be praised for those that have given of their means.

At Harper's Ferry I spent four years and they were years of hard labor, but they were just as sweet as they could well be, for the Lord went with me and I found favor with all of the teachers. When I had spent the first eight months there I learned to have the greatest love for my beloved teachers, and when the time came for me to leave the teachers I thought that my poor heart would break. Though I was coming to my own people in Brooklyn, I felt that I was leaving my best friends on the earth and so did all of the students.

Well, now the Summer had passed and gone and the Fall came when God permitted all of the loving ones to come together once more to take up the cares of studies again. So the time of the winter season was always a blessing to all, and some found it the happiest time of their lives, for they found Jesus precious to their souls and could study so much better than they could before.

CHAPTER IV.

THERE were sometimes as many as sixty or seventy brought to the knowledge of the Truth, and sometimes we had to go out of the classroom into the prayer-room, for the Lord was among us in the Spirit's power.

When in 1886 I went out for good, that I might be of some use to my own people I started in the strength of the Lord, and He did give me the greatest victory as a school teacher, for all of the people sought me to take their children in my school and give them a start. I had my hands full of work, but I let them come in for the Board always sent them to me find out if I could find room and time, and I always made the time for when scholars find that a teacher loves them they will do any amount of hard studying.

And so the time rolled on, with everything to make me feel like hard work, in the strength of the blessed Lord.

I was three years old when I was leaving my own dear mother's home to go to my new mother's home, or I should say to my white mother's home, to live with her, and I left my mother's as happy as any child could leave her own home, for this lovely lady was always at

45

my mother's to see me ever since I could remember anything, and she was the joy of my little life and I seemed to be all the joy of her sweet life. She had learned to love me from the time that I came into the world.

She had watched me in my cradle and longed for the day to come when I should be able to walk, for she knew that I would follow her everywhere she should go. She said to all of the friends around that if I should live to remember her that would be all that she would ask.

And so she read her blessed Bible and prayed until she saw her prayers answered, and then she went to her home in glory, where she has watched and waited and longed to see the good old ships of those who have washed their robes and made them white in the Blood of the Lamb.

I can never tell anyone how many happy hours that I had, for the only trial that I had was that of sickness, which caused me to be of a great care to her all of her life. It was her delight to wait on me and to have her cousin, the doctor, to be always ready to come at any moment she should send for him. He was a good doctor by the name of Sims, and I always liked him, too, until I had the typhoid fever and I had to take some oil. I did not like to take it and he held my hands so that they could pour that in me, and he and I fell out.

My white mother used to give it to me, but she did not let me know what she was giving me, for she put some molasses in the oil and cooked them, so I should not know. I would not have known if I had not seen her one night have the old bottle in her hand putting the oil in the kettle, which she was making ready for me, and I looked up and saw what it was and as young ones will do, did not want to take molasses and butter which I had been taking so long, for I had to take it on every night or I could not speak.

Later on she moved from the place where she was and bought another farm where it was not near the water, as the doctor thought that was not a good place for me to be, and I was not sick so much as I had been at the former.

The first hard spell of sickness on this farm was the fever that I was sick of at the time that she took sick of the yellow jaundice, and she turned as yellow as anything could be. She went home with that awful malady, thinking of me and of what my future should be in God's hands, to love and bless the world in which I should live if it should be the will of Him who knows the future of all the people that live on this earth.

So God has been a father and a loving mother and all else to me, and sometimes there has been enough of trials in this life to make me almost forget that I had this strong arm to save me from these trials and temptations; but when I fly to Him I find all and in all in Him.

He is my rock and my hiding place in the time of trials, for a child that had all of the love and comfort of a queen was now left to her own dear mother, who had so many more and had to work so hard to take care of us all that I have seen sit up all night long working for her little ones. I used to feel sorry to see her sitting up alone at her work. I would get up out of the bed and sit with her till daylight; for I was always near mother after the dear one had been plucked from this earth to await my arrival.

I have found that learning is to refine and elevate the mind, so we should cultivate our hearts and minds and live to bless those we meet. We should neither flatter nor despise those that are rich or great.

It was not long after this dear one had been called away before we were all in different places, and to share the fate that comes to those that are left behind those that have been good and kind. Then the time is coming that mother is to be taken from the whole family of little ones and they are to be left in the hands of others. That is one of the saddest times of life for children when they do not know if they shall ever see her face on this green earth anymore; and if to-day we should hear the cries of those little lambs it surely would break the heart of a stone, for remember that we have the same feelings for our mothers as any race of people and our hearts will melt as easily as the richest ones on this earth.

But God in His great love to us meant that we should see the return of our dear mother to her own and that he would send her and the children out of the Land of Egypt as He did of old when He had tried to teach the rulers how wrong it was to sell and buy human flesh, and this was one of those awful sins that had to be repented of by those that could and would not see the truth. When the wrath of God came upon them and took all of the slaves away from them they could see nothing but tears and curses to the God of Heaven, and some of them cursed the earth, the stars, the moon. The negroes that had prayed so hard to God said that was the cause of the war, for they could see something in their prayers that seemed to reach up to heaven, and the answer had come for their deliverance.

Is not this a great God who can hear the prayers of the faithful ones when they pray? Do not we owe our lives and our all to this great and good God the Father, God the Son and God the Holy Ghost? And if we should fail to recognize Him we should have a worse sin fall on us than ever any one race had.

Well, to my story:

My brother James was my mother's oldest child. He was sent away to the war to keep his master at home, and we did not hear from him for a long time, but we made up our minds that if he did not get killed he would go over to the Northern side as soon as he should get the chance, though we did not see him to tell him to do so, for all of my mother's children were like herself in the love of freedom. My mother was one that the master could not do anything to make her feel like a slave and she would battle with them to the last that she would not recognize them as her lord and master and she was right.

My brother did try to get away, but he was caught and locked up in Richmond, Va., and for a awhile we heard them say that he would be killed, but God was there to help him, so he came out all right and went to work on the breastworks, and when he did try again he got over on the Northern side. They almost caught him again, but as the Lord was his leader at night, he made his escape, and to hear him tell of that river that he crossed and how he walked on the water and he was so scared that he did not know he got wet; but I know that he did get wet, though. He said the Lord carried him over the river without letting him get wet. I am sure that I could not help laughing at my brother to hear of such a thing, for there never was a time that I have read of since the time of Peter that any one was called to walk on the water. The Lord was there Himself to show Peter how small his strength was when he trusted in his own strength, and Peter would have failed entirely if his Lord and Master had not been there.

And so it would have been with my dear brother. He would have been taken by the Southerners, and that would have been his last trial on this side of the grave.

My sister Frances was hired out and we did not see her from one Christmas to the other, for she was a good way off where she could not get home. She was treated very badly by some of those where she lived and her limbs had been sprained so that she could hardly move on them. When later on the Lord had it so arranged that she was taken home to live, where she could be cared for; she soon got better and was able to go about helping mother, with the rest of the children, for my brother who had to help her to care for the children was gone, and she was all the help that my mother had, for I was not large enough to do much and had not been put to mind the children.

The gentleman that my dear brother belonged to was a Methodist and a minister. He did not want to go to the war and so he sent my poor brother to defend what belonged to him, and he did not get the good of it after all, for my brother was determined that he would gain his freedom if he could and he tried and did not get tired of trying.

Then my sister Annie was given to the gentleman's married son and she was not with us, and sister Tempy Green was with the minister, and she was one of the dead ones that mother had a time to get. Maggie, Susie, Martha and Mary were at the same place where mother was sold from, and she went

and got them at once. It was like a dream to
them to see how far she had been sold and to
see her back there again.

Sister Lavinia was at the same place
where I was and she was treated very badly by
the man's own daughter, for she would whip
her without cause. Sister Rosa was at the
same place and she was three and a half years
on mother's return. As I told you, she was six
weeks old when mother was sold and that
made it three years and three months that
mother was gone from her own native home to
a part of the country where she did not know
any one, not even the great God who had been
so good to her all of those years when she was
gone; and all of her whole life God was
watching over her and giving to the world one
child who was to help to educate the down-
trodden race which was, through Abraham
Lincoln, to be God's leader for the children that
were in Egypt in the South, and God with this
leader and the race, they came through fire
and smoke, and now they can see the light of
another day. Some of the race say that they
are sometimes, in their thoughts, ashamed that
they belong to a race that has been in
bondage, but I have never felt that way, for I
am glad that things have been as they were,
for God has moved in a way that is unknown to
men and His wonders He has performed, and

has planted His footsteps in the South, the West, the East and in the North, and is watching the people and asking them what doors are they opening for the Ethiopian.

Father Abraham is calling to the Ethiopians to know what has been the result of the great emancipation, and can we not send the echo back with a jubilee, that we are marching on in education in double file, and longing to see the day that not one of your sons and daughters of this broad earth but what shall learn to read and write; though it may bless the earth with a tenfold blessing that they will not forget to bless God with a hundred fold.

Three cheers for this great Emancipator!

And while he may sleep yonder, forgotten may be by some, his name has a green spot in my heart and shall ever keep green while on this side I stay.

And there is another one who sleeps yonder whom I shall not forget and that is Father John Brown, whose ashes are as dear to me as the apple of mine eye; and how can I forget him after four years of study at the dear old place where he was taken from and hanged, because he saw the wrath of God upon the nation and came forth to save his people.

Another one who will ever be shining bright in the hearts and minds of the whole negro race, and what shall I say of him who led us to the greatest victory the world has ever known--Ulysses. S. Grant, the loved of all nations and the pride of all lands; he whom the world admires, to call the blessed, who mourned for this land to see the end, and God did help him in ways that man knew not, save himself and his God.

And there is another dear one that God will help me to remember with all of the love and gratitude, and it makes me feel sad as I have to speak of her once more and it may be that I shall have to speak of her many times, as she was the one that brought me on to this lovely city, and that is my mother, who has gone to that land of song where there is no more of sickness or sorrow and where God will dry every tear.

There is an another I remember and that is Father Charles Sumner, who for years wrote and also fought and spoke, as never man spoke, for the race and the Civil Rights Bill, that it might not die, but it should be a rock for the defense of the race.

And there is another that I shall not leave out of this book, for if I did the book would be incomplete, and that is Frederick Douglass, the greatest of men among the negro race of this country or of any land on the globe. He wrote and spoke and went all over to try to do all he could for his race, and who could forget such men as these? I would say in true lines, may the earth fail to move sooner than I forget those noble-lives. Honored be their memories and honored be their ashes, for their lives shall live in the memories of all coming generations and their ashes will make rich the soil whereon they lie.

May God give us some more of such men as these for they are few, and we need so many now to go forth and speak the truth.

And there is dear Doctor David Moore, that my pen, I fear, would fail to move, if I did not do him honor. He was beloved and honored to the last day of his stay in the Washington Avenue Baptist Church, and it was on account of sickness that he had to leave this city and go up in the northern part of this State that he might be able to preach the Word, and God did make him well after he had left Brooklyn; and his work has been crowned with great success.

God did use him in this city to His own
glory in saving men, women and children from
the very door of sin and the dread of the life,
which is to come. And may the God of Heaven
and the Ruler of this earth be with him as he
comes near the Jordan to make its waters
calm, and enter in the gate and hear the
blessed "Well done, good and faithful servant,
enter thou in the joys of thy Lord."

J. D. Fulton is one that will have one of
the highest places at God's right hand, for he
started out to look after the Ethiopian's rights
when he was only seventeen years of age.
What can be said of a long life like his, that has
written and traveled and spoke to such large
crowds of hearers in the interest of the race
which I represent. How I have seen those
silvery locks fly as his warm heart melted to
tears as he pleaded for the down-trodden of
the Ethiopians; and if God has ever heard a
prayer I know that He hears the prayer of this
dear good man, for I have seen the answer
come in mighty power, in many ways, to the
saving of precious souls, and the way that he
wrote about the negro in this country and its
problem.

He was called to the Hanson Place
Church to preach and he worked hard, with
God's help, and improved the church and many

were brought to the Savior through the Word, such as the Lord will own and bless at the last day.

Doctor Fulton is one of the best men on this broad earth to love and labor for humanity and I do not think that my race, the noble Ethiopians, should ever forget him as long as God shall spare his life. When the time shall come when the dear blessed one shall be called to the world above, and that active form is stilled in death and when that silvery voice is no longer heard in the defense of the down-trodden Ethiopians and the oppressed of any land, that he will hear the "Well done, good and faithful servant, enter thou into the joy of thy Lord."

And to think of one who has written so long never more to wield the pen in the cause of the church and God's children is a sad thought to the writer, for she has loved him as a father and he shall ever have a green spot in my heart for I shall never forget his kind, words to me in my lonely hours.

Dr. J. D. Fulton's first wife was one of the loveliest women that ever lived, for I have been to their house to dine with the family and I found that Mrs. Sarah Fulton and family were the same that they were in the church. There

was the sweetest home that I ever saw in all
my life, for the father and the mother were all
love, and then take Miss Jennie, the eldest
child, and she was a lovely girl, and there was
Miss Nellie, another lovely girl, and Sadie, the
youngest girl, and she was her father all the
way, and the boy Justin, who came to the
family while I was away. I think he has a large
heart like his dear father, and I do know that if
he only is a good man like his father God will
own and bless him.

Dr. Fulton's second wife, Aunt Laura, was
a lovely woman, for we all learned to love her
when her first husband was living.

Miss L. A. Pousland was one of the best
ladies I have seen in this city, for it was from
her house that I went to the Wayland Seminary
in 1875, and to her love I owe a love of
gratitude, and to all that may come to me as
worldly goods I shall always think of Miss L. A.
Pousland and of her love to me when I was
getting ready for school and the letters full of
love to me all the time while I was prosecuting
my studies. Oh, how she longed to see me out
in the world doing my Master's will and helping
to teach, for she is a Boston lady, and they are
a learned people and like to see all others
learn, and that is the way, like the old Pilgrim

Fathers were, that there should be a grand common level for all after them.

To my story of child in House's family:

This Mr. John House had the largest sum offered to him for a girl as I was that was ever offered for any one and he would not accept the whole world of money, on account of the one that had loved me and cared for me, for he well knew that after all of those prayers that he would be sinning; and he would not have had my mother sold away from her children if his brother would have let him know it in time. He went away to attend court and to his surprise found that my mother was sold. He came home at once to let us know of it, and he was the one that called in my sister Frances and sister Annie and sister Rosa, for the two oldest that I speak of fell to a dead brother who had drank himself to death, and these were sold to pay for his drink. He had been dead for some time and those that he owed now came in to get their pay, which was their only chance; and the money that they got did not do them much good, thanks to God, for it was in the time of the war and the money was of the Confederate money, and it was during the great struggle when this money was called in never more to be the money of these United States, for this Union needs the kind of money that will be

good in all lands, and I am glad that the people
can see it now as they never saw it before.

CHAPTER V.

I AM glad that the dear Lord has laid it in my heart at this time in life to let the world hear something of a life that they will all be filled with a love for one whom it has been a delight to meet at any and all times.

Mrs. Sarah Potter, who is a beloved and dear lady, who is the bright morning star of the Washington Avenue Baptist Church, and who is one of the brightest lights that this city has or ever will have, for she is all over this city looking after the needy ones, comes from a noble family and all of the family have been foreign missionaries. She has been a home missionary for many years and God has blessed her and her labors, and her dear father was doing missionary work in India for fifty years, and God blessed his work there. Now that his dear work has been finished in this world and he has gone to his reward, his works do follow him, for the number that have been saved through his preaching eternity will tell.

His form will no more walk out on the field of battle for the Lord, and who can fill the place of such a life work as this child of the King has filled? And to go home to his beloved and blessed Master with his arms full of blessed sheaves; and as we think of him, how we wonder in our daily walks if we shall go to the Savior with our hands full or shall we go empty-handed and thus to meet our Savior so; not one soul with which to greet Him, must we empty-handed go?

I have heard of Mr. Mason as one of the first to go among the Coreans, and I have seen some of them, that have taken the Lord for their all and in all, come to this land of ours to fit themselves for the blessed work among their own people. God be praised for such a man as Dr. Mason and all of his loving children, who have had the same spirit that their father had, and he was filled with the Holy Ghost and with the power of the Lord.

Mrs. Sarah W. Potter was the beloved wife of a sea captain, Mr. William Potter, and he owned a ship that sailed the Indian Ocean, and he was washed overboard one night while his wife, Mrs. Potter, was sick, and she did not know that he had a watery grave until the next day. They had one son, who is now married, by the name of Frank, whom I held as an idol, as he always called to me when in trouble, for his dear mother taught him the love of the Bible, and he would not fight any boy, let them do him as they would. He knew that I would go after the boys for blocks, as I was one of those soldiers that was not afraid to fight. As he grew older I told him that he had to go out into the world to fight his way and I wanted him to begin it at once, and he did learn to battle for himself. He married a lovely girl by the name of Miss Katie Harvey and they have two children, the eldest a girl and the youngest a boy, which is the lovely little man of the home.

I have seen that mother sit up at nights waiting for her son to come that she might ask a blessing on him before he should sleep, and how could that boy go astray after all these prayers and entreaties? May, he lead his lambs to the blessed Master, and have the "Well done, good and faithful servant, enter thou into the joys of thy Lord."

To my story of work in the City of Brooklyn:

The lady, Miss L. A. Pousland, whom I spoke of in the preceding pages, is the place where I found myself living in 1875, after twelve or thirteen years of service. It was there that I met Mrs. Sarah Potter. She has been all of a mother to me to give me all the encouragement she could bestow on me. For all of this kindness I am more than grateful to my Heavenly Father, for I know that all goodness comes from Him. He surely has shown His love to her in sparing her to see me go from her home to Washington to school and spend three years and then go to Harper's Ferry and spend four years, and to see me out in the world teaching for eleven years, and to break down while at my post and now at home to serve in another way. Is not this not God's love to me, as a poor, humble servant of His? I should never forget to give the love and honor due Him.

God knows my heart and He will bless the work in my hands, as the writer of this book.

When I found that I could get through school in a given time as I had studied hard, if I had the money, I told Miss L. A. Pousland, that I would not be there to work anymore, as I had a place in Saratoga Springs for the Summer. She felt bad to lose me, but as she knew that I could make more money for three months at the Springs she wanted me to have my heart's desire, so I came on from school and went to see her and then made ready for the Springs, getting one of my sisters to go with me and taking such things as we could. We were there too soon and we had to wait for work, and I went around and made myself known to the white people. They soon called on me to come and do work for them, and the first was a Mrs. Carpenter, a good lady. She then got her married daughter to have me to work for her family and they were a fine family. Her daughter's husband was a grand studio man on Broadway, doing a good business. Then she sent me to another friend of hers, and my sister and I could live for a while. When the rush came I did not forget the one who had helped me, but went to her two days out of a week, for she had her house filled with boarders, and the Summer was all a blessing to her and her family.

There was Mrs. Purdy, who was another one of my friends, for I did work for her laundry for three years, and she said whenever I came to the Springs and wanted work to come to her; if the house was filled there was room for me. So you see how God did open the way for me in that strange and lonely place, where there are so many that go there for the Summer looking for work. I went out of the house where we were stopping and got the washing and brought it home to my sister, for she would not go out of the house as she had not been from the place where she lived before. I got her to go with me to help me with the work, and it was coming in so fast I had to get a white lady to help us to get through, for the colored people said that we would not get work as the laws were passed to keep the New York workers out, and I told them that they would have to pass laws to keep the rich people of New York

from coming there to board if they should keep
the workers out; so I did not hear to that, and
found the way for I had the will, and where
there is a will there is always a way. So much
for the first Summer.

Well, the second time I went up alone. I
say alone, I mean that my sister did not go, but
the Lord did go with me that Summer, for I did
not go to the house where my sister and I was
for they tried to discourage us the first time. I
always mark one that is an enemy to me and
shake the dust off of my feet and let the Lord
do for that one what He thinks is best.

Well, for the third year I was there with the
Lord and He was surely there with me. I did not
do any work on the Lord's Day, but tried to
teach them. When they made me an offer of
larger pay for the work done on the Lord's Day,
I told them that in six days the Lord made the
heavens and the earth and He rested on the
seventh day, and I felt that if He needed rest
on that day I was sure that I must have rest. So
the Sunday work was not carried on any more
in that laundry. He said that the Lord had sent
me to that laundry for the bettering of all in it.
The gentleman was from Philadelphia and his
name was Mr. Cheek.

So you see how the Lord preached His word through me, a feeble one of the dust, and what cannot the Lord help us to do if we only trust in Him and if we strive to live for His honor and glory while on this side of Jordan?

Mrs. Purdy had one daughter, and a lovely girl in music, and her name was Kittie Purdy. She was sought to play everywhere as she was a fine player, and everyone thinks her a very pretty girl. Her mother is a perfect lady, for she used to be so kind to her help. She never was late in any of her meals for the help and she always sat down with us and eat with us. She was as jolly as any one at the table and she always called me her bird, for I was on the wing of song from the time I began my work until my work was finished, and then I would start home as happy as anyone could be. Then I would be the first to greet her in the mornings always and she used to say that I brought to her a great deal of comfort each hour and drove all of her business cares away. I used to feel glad that I, although a working girl, could be of some love and comfort to someone, and it makes me feel glad to-day that God in His love to me and for me can own such a feeble one.

My next start was for Asbury Park to do work for Mrs. Haseltine, another lovely lady, who was a Boston lady and whom I learned to love as a mother. I worked for her two years and was to have worked for her the third year if she had not taken sick at the time she did. A gentleman came on from Philadelphia and she got me to work for him and I found him a fine gentleman. I praise God for all that came to me while I was pursuing my studies, and to-day I do feel like saying,

"Blessed assurance, Jesus is mine,
  Oh! what a foretaste of glory divine;
  Heir of salvation, purchase of God,
  Born of His spirit, washed in His blood.

This is my story, this is my song,
  Praising my Savior all the day long,
  This is my story, this is my song,
  Praising my Savior all the day long."

To my story: Mrs. Haseltine, I said, had to go to the Saratoga Springs for the Summer and she used to let me hear from her, but my work in school was so great that I lost sight of her and I do not know if she is in Florida or not. Wherever she is I love her and she has my heart. She did all that she could all the time that I worked for her to let me do extra work for the boarders so that I might earn money outside of what she paid me, and the ladies used to come to the laundry and talk to me, for some of these ladies went to school as I did and some of them waited at the large hotels in the Summer time to pay their board. The gentleman that had Mrs. Haseltine's house took me in at evening time to entertain the guests, and they all helped me. When I came home to make ready for school I was at our own church one evening when dear Dr. J. D. Fulton was giving us one of his grand lectures, and he gave me time to sing, read and speak. The church took a grand collection for me, which amounted to seventeen dollars and seventy-three cents. I was better fixed that year than I had been at any year since I had been going to school, for I had worked all of the Summer and would not spend any of my money as I wanted it all for school, but the evil one came and stole it from me and I was left without a dollar, and I had the heavy heart one is sure to have when they need money as I did. Then I had to borrow money to leave for the school, and you may think how one feels after a Summer's work, and to have someone else to use the money that has not been gotten with their own labor.

Well, I did not know what I should do, so I made up my mind that I had done all that lay in my power--that is, I had earned the money, and someone had taken it from me and I was left to go without. So I took the Lord for it, and could not board as I had done, but I bought some little things to use and boarded myself, and I was up sometimes at the late hours of night, when all of the people were asleep, cooking for the next day, that I might not be late at school. So you can see how loving God was to me.

My life in school was one of joy to me and to my mother and sisters and brother and brothers-in-law, and all of the time that I was in school they were sending me their mites to help me along. My sister, Mrs. E. F. Rodwell and Mr. G. W. Rodwell, and my sister, Mrs. Annie Lindsey and Mr. F. P. Lindsey, were the ones that never for once forgot me, and at Christmas time, I was like a child looking for something. Everybody was good to me. Praise the Lord for all of the love that came to me in the time of need.

Well, my work ended in 1886, though I taught in 1885, and had the blessing of God with me in this school. There were twenty-five out of the school brought to the knowledge of the truth, such as the Lord will own and bless at the last day. God be the glory. Amen and Amen.

A Slave Girl's Story

The place was Woodstock, Shenandoah County, Va., and I was called from that school to go West where they needed me to teach in a place where the teachers had made the pupils almost hate to go to a school. My heart was in that work, which no one liked, so I went there trusting in the Lord. I lost that place, but they got me another one where they built me a new house, and the Lord did bless me in this place, although. I was not able to go to the Baptist Church only once a month, for there was not any nearer than ten or fourteen miles. When the next year came I helped the people build a church and it was all paid for before I left there. How God did pour out His spirit there in the salvation of souls, and He did add unto the dear church such as will be saved at the day when He shall come to make up his jewels; and I can praise His name for such a Savior.

Well, to my story: As a teacher in the same place for eleven years, or I should say I was connected with the same school for that length of time, and all the way the Savior led me. Sometimes it was not all flowers and sweetness, but in it all I can see the hand of the Blessed One, and it used to make me say to myself, Praise the Lord, Oh, my soul, and all that is within me praise His holy name!

After being there for some time I was taken sick and was there sick and could not teach my school for that Winter. It made me feel very bad, but my good Dr. Ford said that he thought all of the county were sorry to learn of my illness and all were losing a good teacher. I would not be able to do any schoolwork for some time to come as the nerves were all overworked, and that had brought on other troubles, which were of a dangerous nature. So my heart was heavy indeed, and if I had not had my hope built in Jesus Christ I would not have stood, for I felt that all other ground was to me a sinking sand. I stayed there all of the Winter and then came on home to Brooklyn, and the Lord was so good to make me well; I went back to my work and taught all that Winter, and when my school was out I then went down to the county seat, which is ten miles from the station and is about fourteen from my school, where I spoke of.

Hinton is a lovely little town on the Chesapeake and Ohio Railroad and in the Blue Ridge and Alleghany Mountains, and is one of the greatest places on the road, as all of the trains from the West, East, South and North stop there. It is a lovely town and they have a roundhouse there where they build locomotives. They have a fine Y. M. C. there. There are a number of men employed at this place. They have two nice Baptist Churches and a Baptist Mission, two Methodist Churches, one Episcopalian, one Congregational, one Presbyterian and one Roman Catholic and one college, a number of private schools and a number of public schools and the county is doing a good work in education, and to the Lord be all the praise for all of this good work.

Hinton I said was a lovely place. Like Harper's Ferry, that I spoke of in the preceding chapter, it is situated on Camp Hill in a lovely place, between the Potomac River on one side and the Shenandoah River on the other, and it has two of the most beautiful bridges I ever saw. When you see the trains coming and going it looks lovely.

The Wayland Seminary is in a lovely spot on Meredian Hill, between Fifteenth and Sixteenth streets, and you can see all over the City of Washington. It is lovely to behold with all of its fine buildings and art galleries, though I do not like it as well as Harper's Ferry, for I was not well the whole time I was there and I had so much better health at the Ferry. I bless God that I made the change when I did or I might have been gone to my long home before I had the time to see so much of God's love to me in the way He has led me through paths that I did not see then. I can truly say unto Him, Lord, Thou hast been my dwelling place in all of these years of trial and has been my rock in a weary land and my shelter in the times of storm.

Well, I came home last October a year ago, 1895, and made up my mind to stay for the time being. Some of the people found out that I was here and they sent for me to come to see them. I went to Mrs. Murphy's the next week and I was there nearly a year and found that I could not do much lifting, so I did not feel well for quite a while, and I had a heavy day of it the last time that I was there. So I told her daughter I should not come any more as I had gone early that I should get home early. It was nearly six o'clock when I stopped. They are a lovely family of four men and four girls, all of whom are very fine indeed; two sons married, and children, and one daughter married and she has two little ones. Miss Josephine is a schoolteacher, Miss Alice is the housekeeper, as the mother is not very well at times. One of the lovely girls is a Sister in a convent.

I also did work for her daughter, Mrs. Nellie Chester, and she is a lovely woman. I had to lose her work as she had to get her a girl.

I also worked for fine families by the names of Mrs. Handford and Mrs. Taylor, but they went away from this city.

CHAPTER VI.

I AM now doing work for a lovely family by the name of Mrs. Coddington, as her husband has died not long since, and he was a nice man and they have two lovely girls that teach school. I also work for Mrs. White, who is a lovely lady, and all of her family.

At the Pells and the Powells. Mrs. Pell is a lovely woman, with two children, one a lovely young lady and full of the sweetest music the ear ever heard, for I do not think that there ever was any one that could play sweeter music than her. The other is a boy, a nice youngster of promise.

Mrs. Powell is the sister of the first Mrs. Pell and she has one daughter, who is a Mrs. Pell, whom I have to call Mrs. E. Pell to let each one know which one I mean. There are other ladies in the mansion that are very nice to me. Mrs. Pell No. 1 is the head of the house and is a fine lady, and in telling you of those that I have worked for and I am doing work for I mean to tell that it is by the day that I work for some of them; as you will see as you read this that I have had very few places where I lived out by the month, and staying a good while in a place.

I did work for Mrs. Johnson, but as her business is not so good at times, she has me whenever she can feel as if she can spare the money. So this little life of mine has been almost locked up in a nutshell, and Jesus has come to me in the spirit's power that I should tell the world of His wonderful love to me a poor sinner of the dust. And what cannot the Lord do for those who put their trust in Him? We feel like saying to the blessed One, how amiable are all of Thy works, oh Lord, and our eyes are seeing Thy salvation in many parts of the earth.

I can remember the first time that it was my pleasure to hear dear Dr. J. D. Fulton. It was on Thanksgiving Day when he first came to this city to preach at the Hanson Place Church, as their pastor. The Rev. David Moore had him to preach the Thanksgiving sermon at the Washington Avenue Baptist Church, and we were all delighted at hearing him on that day. I loved him on hearing that sermon, for I felt the spirit power on that day, through his preaching. I shall always think of the Doctor and his loving family, for we, as the negro race, have not such a friend on earth as Dr. Fulton. I am not afraid to say it to his dear honor is he is not dead, and I wish every negro knew him as I do for then they would all feel toward him as I feel. I hope that he will long live to tell the truth as he has in days gone by; and if he was in this city where the evil is so strong, we should hear him sounding the watchword, and that is the reason that those that loved the ways of sin did not like him, for they felt that he had cause to trouble them while they were yet in their sins.

But I hope that the day will come when. I shall hear him again in this city, and I hope that God will give him long life and that he may see the travel of his soul and be satisfied, for, I know that he tries to do God's will in this love that he has for humanity and that is why the Lord will bless him in all the work that his hands find to do.

I was not at home when he left this city and I felt sad when I found that he was gone, for we shall ever miss him. My prayer is to God that he may live to a good old age and that when he shall be called to come up higher that he may be caught up in the air to meet his Lord and Master and all of those that have gone on before, and be ready to Crown Him King of Kings and Lord of Lords.

PROGRESS OF CHURCH WORK.

A speech to a crowded church, in the year of our Lord 1888, in Talcott, Summers Co., W. V. I was asked to have this published out there, but I wanted to have it brought to my home in Brooklyn. I was into so much work out there, and my people were not there to see what the Lord did help me to do:

Dear friends, we are here to-night to commemorate this grand occasion, and our watchword is Onward and Upward to the Prize!

This is a time that we should all shout the Jubilee and to send the glad tidings to all the world and to let all the nations know that we are on our march to that happy land of song.

Dear friends, let us look for a few moments and think of the time when you had not a church where you could worship God. I told you that God would give you this lovely place, where no one could drive you out, and to see what great things He has done for you in a little time, and how great things can He not do if we will only trust Him? We have those of our race that have held places of greatest trust and God bless them in those places. Why should we give up the fight and lay our armor by when there is so much for us to do? No, no, we cannot and we will not lay the grand old armor down, for the Lord is on our side and we shall surely conquer if we look to Him whose arm is so large and strong. Then let us take fresh courage and march on until we reach the goal, and then we shall be glad and rejoice for the Lord has spoken good to His people, the Ethiopians.

Oh, ye colored people, why not take this as yours and begin now to rejoice ye in your own race and feel proud of the race, but not ones that can dance the best on the ball-room floor, for there is very little in that when it is all summed up in a whole. Let us thank all the good people who have shown any love to us while we have been in this work of building and may they all find favor in the sight of God. You have a dear good pastor who is willing to give his life to the Lord and the church. Let us take fresh courage and march into His service, for we shall gain if we only trust in God and do the right He will help us to persevere.

Time would fail me and my pen would fail to move if I should try to enumerate all of the blessings that have come to us as a race. I hope that we, as the hated negro race, will make a fresh start from this night and do all that we can to forward the work in this church, and God will send us a blessing.

A Slave Girl's Story

ETIQUETTE OF YOUNG MEN.

I was wondering a few days since if the men of the present day had lost the respect that men used to have for the women. I was carried back to the year of 1884 while in school with so many of the young men of my own race, when I saw so much of the respect that they showed to us girls and that was what caused me to write this to their honor. I think that true etiquette is one of the greatest blessings that young men can have for the women, for it is to them that we look to for the protection and love, and if we fail to find it in them where shall we look? This is one of the greatest fortunes that one can have, and it is that which makes a young man what he ought to be. We, as the women, need so many of such ones and the world needs them fully as much, and the God who made them looks for more and when he does not find it in the dear creatures that He has made it makes Him feel sad.

I found a number of young men that used to attend the Wayland Seminary that had the greatest regard for the girls, and I could not but notice them in this respect and their kind acts while there, although I was not in the same classes with them, but I never saw them make any difference while I was in school. I always found good friends among them and I never saw a young man meet one of the young ladies but they lifted their hats, and that made the people of Washington, D. C., always speak of it in the kindest terms. One never loses anything in this way, and their virtues are greater than gold.

When the weather was very bad one day and I was coming from school and a young man saw me fall down, he came to help me home and I felt very grateful, and I feel that wherever that young man shall go he will have favor in the eyes of all, and God will be his leader for he has made a good beginning.

SCHOOL LIFE.

While at the Harper's Ferry school I found the loveliest teachers that ever were in a school. Professor Brackett, the head of the school, is a fine gentleman, and his wife, Mrs. W. Brackett, is a lovely lady and she is one of the finest teachers that ever lived. She has three nice children, two of them are girls and one boy, who is a young man by this time, for I have not seen him since he went to Maine to attend school, which is the Bates'. It is a fine school of Latin, and a number of the students went to that same school.

Mr. W. P. Curtis was one of the professors. He was my Sunday-school teacher and he was fine.

Mr. D. M. Wilson was a dear professor, whom we loved. Miss Caroline Franklin was a lovely teacher and we all loved her. Miss C. Brackett was one of the lovely teachers, and one whom every one of the other teachers loved, for she was one of the finest readers that ever lived, let it be man or woman. They used to have her read nearly every afternoon when the school was out, and sometimes they would call to Professor Curtis to read to the school. He was a very good reader, but Miss C. L. Franklin was the grand trainer of the

85

whole school. They had a grand reading circle there at nights for the rich of the Ferry, and she was the one to do the fine reading. All of the noble people of the place loved her and she will ever be loved and remembered by all who knew her. She is now in Washington, D. C., teaching, and the people have learned to love her as we did. I do not think that anyone could help loving her for her love and fidelity to the race, which she represents.

Miss C. L. Franklin's mother, who is a lovely woman whom we all love as a mother, for she had many of the students at her house to board, like Mrs. William Lovett, and she was so very kind to all of them that she will be remembered by us all, for we love those in our school life that would say a kind word to us. It was to help us along in our daily toil.

Mrs. Julia Robinson was one of the lovely ladies at the Ferry, also, and all of the teachers boarded there. She has a number of the students that board with her and she is much beloved.

Mrs. Bell was one of the ladies that kept boarders and she is much beloved. Mr. W. M. Bell is one of the teachers and all love him as a teacher.

Mr. J. Trinkle; who keeps one of the halls in the Summer time has a number of boarders, and does well all of the Summer months and in the Winter, he teaches in or near the Ferry. With it all they are all doing what they can to help to forward the interest or an education in all of that section, and I really think that part of the country will show a larger percentage of those that have been educated through the churches than could have been taught in the public schools, for the terms are so very short that it is hard for the people to get a start.

But God has wonderfully blessed the teachers that have been sent on there from the North to look after the interests of the negroes. They love the work of the schoolroom, and it is their meat and their drink daily to give away what they have received. The Word says that it is more blessed to give than to receive, and we are always ready to receive from the hands of our earthly friends, and it is much greater to receive from God.

Mr. Thomas Lovett has two lovely little girls, named, respectively, Florence, the eldest, and the other Shoelett, and they are very smart. Mr. Lovett has built a hilltop house in a lovely place. It is filled in the Summer time, while he has music for the boarders. That makes it pleasant during the warm weather of the Summer months, and it is one of the loveliest places that can be found on the B. & O. Railroad, and the white people go their from all parts.

I had the pleasure of stopping there on my way home in 1895, and it did my soul good to find such a fine house built by one of the colored gentlemen and one that I had known; for I was at his mother's boarding house for the whole time that I was at the Ferry. He was teaching school then in the Wintertime and looking after his mother's business in the Summer time. So I am glad that some of my people are trying to make an honest living. He is one among the many at the Ferry that are keeping boarding houses; and I am thankful for all that comes to us as a race. I hope, as I have often heard dear Dr. Fulton say that he wanted to see the race go forward, and I pray that the time is not far distant when all of the friends of the negroes shall see them making men and women of themselves, and then the grand problem will be solved. Then we shall be glad, for I am grieved night and day for my own people, and I feel so grateful to God for letting me see and to know that I have such a good friend as Dr. Fulton is. He shall be loved by me as long as I live, and I hope that he will ever be loved by all that shall read this life of mine, for he has been a father to me and I am one that always remembers a kindness as long as anyone will do one for me. God will bless those that will think of me in love.

As this day has been one of quiet to me, I have wondered what it would be to me if I could look into those bright mansions above and see my two mother's faces. What a joy there would be at the sight of them seeing me and of me seeing them, and we all singing,

Holy, holy, holy, Lord God Almighty.   Early in the morning, our songs shall rise to Thee; Holy, holy, merciful and mighty,   Casting down their golden crowns around the glassy sea.

And what a glory it will be for all that have washed their robes and made them white in the blood of the Lamb; and I know that two darling mothers have washed their robes and made them white, and to God be all the praise for the great love that He has shown to poor me, who feels so lonely on this lovely Lord's day. How much have I found in His service, too, and if I could be able to go there to-night I feel that I should be blessed, but I have to stay at home to-night as I have not been well for a month or more. I feel grateful as can be that I could be out this morning, and I will pay vows unto my God as long as I shall live, for He is my rock and my hiding place in the time of trouble. I have had a storm of them and it is to Him I fly to shield my soul from the evil one, and knowing as do how many hard spells I have had, it is right for me to be as careful as I can, taking the Lord for my healer. How He has blessed me so many times when there were no other hopes for me to build on, I have found that I could trust in His almighty power.

I shall not forget the kind care of Dr. Matthews, of this lovely city, whom God gave to me when I was very low and the three times a day that he paid his visits to see how I was getting along. He was so kind in his words to comfort me and to give my mother cheer I shall always think of him kindly, for the snow was so deep that a horse could not travel very well and he had to walk it three times a day. I had not my white mother then to care for me, but my own mother did what she could for me and I know that she has her reward in heaven for all that she has ever done for me in the times when I needed the most care.

There is good Dr. Reeves, a good Quaker doctor, and I had to have him to attend me. He was very kind and gentle in his treatment of me and I am very glad that I found such a friend in him, for he was like a father to me? I shall not overlook dear Dr. Warmsley, who was a good doctor to me and he was kind as he could be, and I shall not forget him, although I have not seen him for a long time.

What shall I say of the last doctor that I was under out West, and that is Dr. J. W. Ford, who was so kind to me as a stranger. He would come when he was sent for. It made no difference what time of day or night. It might be you would find him on his way where he was sent for and sometimes he would be on the road all night long, for he is the best doctor in the county, and I was going to say the best in the State of West Virginia. They all send for him, far and near, where they have any fever, and he is so good in fevers, through the Lord, he is sure to bring them out of if they do as he tells them. May the Lord give him a good long life to do the will of Him who is the greatest doctor after all. And if we only put our trust in Him we shall find that He will make our sick bed easy for us and He will carry us all the way while we are sick, for He has borne our sorrows and sickness.

To my story as a schoolgirl: It was full of sweet love and regard, for I gained favor with all of the teachers and professors and all of the pupils. The Lord be praised for all of this love and joy that came to me in my school days. Then the love that came from the Washington

91

Avenue Baptist Church of sending me the sum
of twenty or thirty dollars to help me in paying
my expenses was of the greatest love for one
in a school, as I wanted to pay as I went, and
then the Sunday-school would send me their
money, one of the dear, loving favors of God's
love, and naming each time from which the
money came and sending it through the Board
at Chicago. Then Mrs. Conley or Mrs. Connell
sent it to me and the Board sent the same way
when my own beloved church sent me money.
It was in the time of Mrs. Sarah Fulton and she
did not forget me when I was in school. The
Mission Band of our church sent me some
money every year after the first year that I went
to school. Sometimes it was to the answer of
my prayers that the money came at the time I
needed it to pay my board and God be praised
for those who from the bottom of their hearts
contributed in the grand and good work of
education. For all that I shall do in this life to
help someone that needs help, I shall think of
the Lord's love to me and try and do what I can
to bring them to the Lamb of God that taketh
away the sins of the world, and to God I owe
my life and my all, and if I should fail to love
and honor Him I know that He will not
remember me before His dear Father in
heaven.

Mr. William Lovett, the father of a large family, is one of the finest gentlemen anywhere around the whole country, and is much beloved by all who know him. The white people who board with him in the Summer time all liked him, for he was so nice and quiet. He has a large family of girls and boys and all are smart. He sent two of them to the Hillsdale College when they had finished at the Ferry, and one was John Lovett, who studied law, and the other one, Miss Etta Lovett, was a fine schoolteacher and a music teacher.

I have just learned that the last one of the girls has married, and that is the youngest of the family. They all have good partners for life, which does not come to all large families. God bless such a father and mother, who have taken such good care of the training of their children.

Mr. John Lovett was one of the teachers of whom I shall speak of, as I boarded in their house for four years. A more lovely woman never lived than his mother. She is known far and wide as one of the best ladies to keep boarders and she has a lovely family of girls and boys. Mr. Thomas Lovett is a schoolteacher and much beloved. He married a doctress, who is one of the finest ladies that lives, She is from the North and she has some

93

of the best people of the Northern cities that she waited on, and they love her to day for the kind care that she had for them.

Miss Emma Carter is one of the teachers, and Miss Lizzie Sims, Miss Frances Sims, Mr. Burrell and Mr. C. H. Plummer; and of later years Miss Mary Brackett has gone there as one of its teachers and there are others that have gone there as teachers. The dear good work is going on in the strength of the Lord and I hope that He will still bless his work. The same that I said of Miss C. L. Franklin I will say of Miss Lulia Brackett, who is married now and is still one of its beloved teachers. She loves the work of teaching the negroes better than her own life and all that she has in Maine. God bless those dear teachers, as they labor there for my own dear people whom God has blessed in getting an education.

Miss Lulia Brackett married a Mr. Loughtner, who is a schoolmaster for the whites at the Ferry, and who is a fine schoolteacher and whom the people like very much. It is a joy to meet him on his way to his schoolhouse.

Mr. William Bell is one of the teachers whom we all love dearly, and he taught school outside for a while before he came to teach at the college. He had the greatest success as a teacher. May God bless those faithful ones as they are far from their homes, family, friends and loving ones.

I had the pleasure of working for a fine family in Brooklyn by the name of Davis, and I found them all a lovely family. I had the pleasure of going away in the country one Summer to a place called Flemington, N. J., and we had a fine time as it was his father and mother's home, and they had a dairy farm and all of the nice things that one finds in the country. I was not well while there as it was low land, and one of their daughters was not well, so I feeling that I would be better to come home they got ready and come on home, and I left them and went to my home where I could rest. In the Fall I was so much better that, I was able to go back out West and take up my work again. When I had finished my public school I taught a pay school for the Summer and had a large number of scholars, and they progressed well. Some of them would go without their food all day to study extra lessons.

It would be all of a joy to the whole world to have seen how well all of the girls, boys, young men and young ladies did in all of the schools where I have had the pleasure of teaching.

I have never taught in any school with any other teacher or teachers, and I was so much more blessed, for all teachers have a way of their own. The new teacher always makes so much change in a school and in the pupils, I found that to do good work in school I should stay long in one place, that I might bring the scholar near to me. Sometimes I have had it rough, but in it all I can see the hand of God leading me to do all that I could to help forward the great cause of education in those parts where there was so much need.

I have just learned that the Rev. J. D. Fulton has had a stroke and I cannot tell how he is at this time, but I cannot do any work until I hear from him, as I have had my mind on him for some time, as he was somewhere in Massachusetts and I had not heard from him for some time. The last time that I heard from him, he was not well, and I knew that he was so great for working that I feared he would break down.

So I wrote to Mrs. Wamsley, his daughter, and shall wait to hear how he is, for I know she will let me know at once as she is there with her father.

I have heard from her and he is better, thank God, and not dead, as so many thought, for he does so much work that, no one thought that he could get over it.

And here on this 20th day of January I fell sick myself and have not been able to take up my work until the 4th day of March, and once more in the strength of the Lord I have taken up this work and hope to push it as fast I can, and I hope to finish it in the near future if the Lord wills. I hope that all who will may have the pleasure of knowing of something of the joys and of the sorrows that have crowned this little life of mine, but in and through it all, I have seen the blessed hand of Him who is wise.

March 4th, 1897.

www.ingramcontent.com/pod-product-compliance
Lightning Source LLC
Chambersburg PA
CBHW052059270326
41931CB00012B/2817